A Pound Of Dirt

poems by

Scarlet Colsen

Finishing Line Press
Georgetown, Kentucky

A Pound Of Dirt

ACKNOWLEDGMENTS

Grateful acknowledgment to the editors of the following magazines where
where some of these poems first appeared: *Chronogram, The Plough
Quarterly*, and *awostingalchemy.com.*

Thanks to Frank Kosempa for his loving help and encouragement, and to
my daughter Ali Zacker Gale, my grandchildren Zoe Gale and Natasha Gale,
as well as Cassandra Quackenbush, Priscilla Lenes, Anna Lenes, Marilyn
Cassotta, and my oldest friend Tina Mueller for their inspiration. Thanks
also to Cara Stewart and Tom Camilleri for their assistance, and to Diane
Cowles, the poet who urged me to write in the first place many years ago.

Publisher: Leah Maines
Editor: Christen Kincaid
Cover Art: "Used" (detail) by Scarlet Colsen;
      Frank Kosempa/ PHOTOGRAPHER
Author Photo: Frank Kosempa/ PHOTOGRAPHER
Cover Design: Elizabeth Maines

Printed in the USA on acid-free paper.
Order online: www.finishinglinepress.com
      also available on amazon.com

Author inquiries and mail orders:
Finishing Line Press
P. O. Box 1626
Georgetown, Kentucky 40324
U. S. A.

Table of Contents

"you gotta eat a pound of dirt before you die"

Ella Moore, my Mamaw

Kemper County, Mississippi

New Knowledge

New knowledge
when old
is like seeing the butterfly
for the first time
when young.

Wild Sleep

I fall asleep to the Canada Geese,
not exactly soft music
and wake at five to their loud, low hurricane.

Surprised that I slept,
remembering the soft slip of its fall,
don't they ever stop singing and playing,
their voices filled with knowing excitement
something
I can only guess at.

Are they singing songs of spring
while I still lie bloated with winter,
as deep and heavy
as snow pushed over and plagued with pebbles
and melting mud?

They have wisdom to give,
these geese who mate for life
and live to seventy.

I think I shall lie and listen
to their joyous Eric Dolphy
and not get up until hell freezes
and heaven gets hot.

First Do No Harm

I feel this very small stranger dancing inside me
dancing a great-escape dance
a war dance
doing experimental dance
pushing
kicking
doing any kind of dance imaginable to find the way out—
the right limb
or hand
or head
or through the heart.

Maybe I could help her—
operate carefully
gently
with sharp rituals
to set her free.

She is not a complete stranger.
I have felt her several times before many years apart
and she knows she has a great gift to give me,
but needs more space to grow
fresh air to breathe
a river
and I need to give her this but I don't know how.

It should be as simple as saying abracadabra
while waving a magic wand.

But her dance is as elusive as the hummingbird's.

Abandoned Collage

I see my depression on the floor, in the dustballs huddled close
to the overflowing laundry bag.
I hear it sneaking in and under my shoes,
and in the leaky toilet when I drag myself from bed
to pee.

Getting water in the kitchen I see it on the table—

"Depression With Feather, Stamp, Stone, Button, Broken Mirror,"

the abandoned collage dressed in dust.

Because it's angry and neglected,
I hear it's plotting to lift itself up and crush me.
Stay away from this room.

I see my depression in the telephone I can't pick up.
What would I say to a friend
after telling them about the pain in my hands,
exhaustion in my body, this pain and depression
so mingled
so twisted
that it leaves me dull,
distorted.

I return to my haven,
my prison,
my bed,
and look at the broken nails
on these hopeless, useless hands.
I reach for a cigarette on the table,
and feel repulsion for the dead day lilies
in murky,
putrid water.

Forget the cigarette.

Smash the vase.

Checked Out

You want to know what makes me sad?
That dying Christmas Cactus over there.
That probably amuses you—I can tell by the way
you just turned away
that it does.

You know, once I had sixty-seven plants,
all healthy,
I loved them,
I loved to take care of them.
Yeah, be a wise ass,
go ahead,
but you asked me—
you're the one that said: "I think you've checked out,"
while I was thinking it was something more like
becoming catatonic.

But then I laugh,
a hysterical laugh.

I'm thinking how much this feels like a Raymond Carver story,
I laugh some more,
Christ, I was living Carver stories before he was born—
that's a lie—
but at least before he was published.

Will You Tell Me?

He told me to sit down and write
I said I would
really, I would.
I wasn't just going to go to sleep.
I could write in bed
I didn't need a chair.

So I stare at the box the Madam Alexander doll came in,
the doll I gave my daughter for Christmas in 1970.
It's fifteen years later and the box looks good.
If you didn't know, you'd say it was two, three years old.
It holds Christmas ornaments now.
There's a whole stack of boxes holding ornaments taking up
half the damn room,
stealing my interest,
making me think about hauling them up to the country.
It felt like yesterday, but it's been nine months since Christmas
and what's the point of hauling them up
just to bring them back?
But I'm always moving boxes and still not unpacked—
two years of my life in boxes too.

So how the fuck am I supposed to write
when my brain jumps around from Ali at five
to divorce
to a body cramped with pain?

How can I write with thoughts as disorganized as this room?
Will you tell me Smarty?
Will you goddamn tell me please?

Thirty-Fourth and First

I am now on the Vertical West Side Highway.
Cars have changed into bumper-to-bumper people.
You move at a rate of a half-a-step or shuffle,
or simply wiggle one foot
so you can pretend you're going somewhere.

It has been an hour and a half now, since you left home.
You are pretending to climb the stairs
to get to the escalator
to get to your third and last train.
You push "What-Am-I-Doing-Here" down
for the eighth, eighteenth, what-does-it-matter time.
You are on your last bumper-to-bumper
and begin to see the light.

Thirty-Third and Park.

You get your coffee and make your decision:
something sweet or something healthy:
brain muffin or pain au chocolate.

Thirty-Fourth and Lex.

Now I'm passing the seedy hotel passed every other Thursday
four months in a row.
The only reason for being here
to photograph the sadness in its face.
Again I do not do it.
Again I have not brought the camera.
Again you think: "What Am I Doing Here?
Do you think you can combine art and cleaning?
There is no time for photographs.
No time for art."

You are predictably late once again.

You light a cigarette.

Thirty-Fourth and Third.

You slacken your pace.

Thirty-Fourth and Second.

You think about your lie,
the lie you tell yourself bumper-to-bumper,
the lie you continue to tell others:
that it would be a good way to make some money,
that you would be alone, no people, no distractions,
a necessity for artists,
necessary for me,
all alone to create as I cleaned.
Didn't I always clean when I needed to think something through?
What Am I Doing Here?

Thirty-Fourth and First.

Dust

Rubbing my finger along the top of a picture frame
the rocker on the bentwood chair
dust everywhere.

The walk to the closet to throw out everything
the green silk blouse
from 1976—
can't do it.

Plagued by the thought,
consumed by the desire to get rid of
to lighten up
to breathe freer
is it all a delusion?
Emptying the closet will bring me all this?

The lone finger making a path of dust-free desk,
leaving the rest…

Back to the closet,
walking out again
empty-handed
head full of failure
sad…

For now, I can only collect a finger-full of dust to throw away.

I Know Better

I lie in this bed
head covered
hiding
buried

some call it
depression

I know better

I can see the eyes of self-loathing
taste its bitter smile
especially in the dark
and smell its foul stare
six inches under.

Gabardined Legs

You say "embrace my fear"
but I'm afraid to do that,
afraid it will encompass me
totally and swiftly
like an ice cream cone consumed
before it can drip
one drop.

This fear...
Where did it come from?
When did it start?

If only embracing my fear
was as simple and easy
as embracing my mother's
gabardined legs when told to say
"How do you do"
to the stranger.

Imprinted

I learn my lesson well,
beaten into me with a switch of my choice
a pussy willow
forced
then into my Mother's hand.

I am my Mother's daughter.

But then away from her,
I became my own person,
a fervent anti-war protester
then a radical feminist
out there
speaking out
shouting out our differences.

And then when she is old
I return under her wing
with no agreement from me,
and I am lost again.

Oh what magic—what power
a mother has over her young
sometimes
most times
always.

She imprints herself again
with the memories she's lost
victims of denial
banging on the door of my sleep
with tight hard fists.

Self-Esteem In Progress

I am a woman of low self-esteem
and don't want to be anymore.

I've hung my mother's shit in plastic bags
        on silver safety pins
        all over my body
and I can't sustain its weight and stench
        its drag and pull
that I can't get up out of bed anymore,
paralyzed by the weight,
crawling,
flat on the floor,
barely able to lift my hand
tearing them away
one by one
starting my life all over
once again.

I lay my pen down...

Better finish rinsing the antique wedding dress
soaking in the bathroom sink.
Better to scrape the cat food dishes
soaking in the kitchen.

I don't want to write these mean hard words down...

I am a woman of low self-esteem
and don't want to be
anymore.

My Papaw's hands were glued to my body
and I know it will hurt when I rip them off
one by one,

like a thousand bandages pressed on hairy places
that have to come off sooner or later—
but no more painful than my Mamaw's eyes,
so knowing
so blind
so scared.

What Do You Want To Be When You Grow Up?

I never told you what to be,
"Just happy," I said,
"I just want you to be happy",
but I never showed you how.
"What do you want to be when you grow up?"
"A doctor," I said,
"Well,"—(long pause, bright smile, pure Mother)—
"How about a nurse?
Then you could marry a Doctor!"

No, I wasn't going to do that to you.
I just wanted you to simply be happy,
but I never showed you how
and my mother never showed me.

I never told you what to be,
"Just independent," I said,
as I replaced one man after the other
just like my mother did,
leaving no time for dust to gather
growing no wings of my own.

No, I never told you what to be,
"Just strong," I said,
but I never showed you how.
"I just want you to be happy, independent, and strong," I said,
as I simultaneously hid my strength even from myself.

Pants On Fire

You're getting double messages,
sunlight streaming in the kitchen window
warming you,
bathing away all fear
while the nasty voice on the telephone
makes it otherwise when you begin
your feeble lies.

Across the room
the beautiful glaring face
makes it otherwise too—
the wise eight year old
who means more to you
than the sun of god chants softly,
hissing out "Liar...
            Liar...
            Liar..."
while her face says so much more
directed at you as straight as an arrow
as clear as the curve behind the sign of danger
no quiet hiss,
screaming instead: "You hypocrite,
                    you deceiver,
                    you betrayer of truth!"

Your daughter's disgust hits hard—
it wounds you more than the voice on the phone,
more than your anger at the one responsible,
the one who bought the hundred dollar shirt
for the hundredth time
instead of paying the phone bill,
the electric bill
the water bill
the silk shirt not for her
not for you
but for him and him alone.

You hang up and pass on to her
the lies you have to tell yourself:
"A little white lie,
it's different than other lies, honest
it is—
sometimes you have to tell one
for water and light
in your life."

You stand there in the bright sunlight
telling her the complete opposite of what
you really want to say,
instead of what you know she wants to hear: "Come on,
let's pack,
let's leave this immoral, selfish bastard
so I can get my values back
be myself proudly,
for me
and most of all
for you."

I Stand and Watch Closely

This Spring you're determined to stay in sync with nature,
is that it?

Both of you resisting your awakening?

Are you afraid that when your bud becomes a full-blown flower
you too will start to die again?

I stand and watch closely,
as if my desire for your growth alone
could pull the flowers up out of the frozen ground,
could matter and make it happen
when what I really want to do is be the bad doctor,
pulling and forcing the birth
too soon.

But too soon is not soon enough.

I don't want to sleep the death sleep with you,
but I don't know how to come alive again
without you and the flowers agreeing.

Yes, you held your joy in your arms,
now you can no longer pick her up.
Disabled, distancing, forgetting, hostile.
What happened in between?
What abyss did you fall into
and cannot crawl out of?

The pain killers engrave your soul.

For Change Sake

If you'da asked me thirty years ago I'da said:
    "I ain't got no father."

If you'da asked me twenty-five years ago I'da said:
    "I don't know him;
    He left when I was two."

Then twenty years ago maybe I'da told you:
    "That bastard—
    you want to know what that prick did?
    He picked up my sister and I
    and dumped us at his parents—
    maybe we'd see him once,
    twice,
    before he'd drive us back again.

    We'd be playing under the house—
    he'd come home drunker'n'a skunk and start yelling
    "Get out from under that house,
     get the hell out from under that house
     'fore I beat the shit outa ya."

    I'm real scared but I come on out.
    My sister, she won't.
    "Please don't hit her—
    Please, please don't!"
    And I'm yelling this at his pant leg I'm pullin on."

'Nother time I'm in the library lookin at the picture album:
under each picture was '6 Months', '8 Months', 'Year and a half',
me and my sister,
it was the very first time I saw myself as a baby.

Then I hear him stumbling up the stairs.
I go out and say: 'Daddy, can I have these baby pictures?
(I don't tell him my mamma told me to get them)

"No!" he yells, waving me away,
        "get the hell away from me. No,
            you can't have no goddamned pictures,"
and that was the last time I saw him,
when I was eight,
when I was too young to know
that I just could have stolen them."

If you'da asked me fifteen years ago, perhaps I'da said:
"You know what that fuckin bastard did?
Out of the blue, when I'm fourteen,
I get this letter from him.
First time I ever got a letter from him,
and he tells me he's in a drunk's home—
        you'd call it rehab today—
but he's bitchin and moanin your poor daddy,
he's all alone
he's hurt
'n he wants me to feel sorry for him."

I rip and tear that letter up into teeny
itsey-bitsey little pieces."

Ten years ago, you really won't believe this one,
"My father", I'da said—
        ("you ain't gonna believe this—
            you just ain't gonna believe
            what that fuckin bastard did now.)—
He married my second cousin.
She's got two kids by another marriage.

One day, they take the kids to the neighbors and say:
'Would ya watch 'em while we go to the store?'
Next thing those neighbors heard,
they were in California."

You ask me about my father?

I'd say the only thing he's good at
is leaving his kids.

Five years ago, I'da told you that I finally got my mother
to talk some about my father.
I had to ask her.

She said I remembered wrong.
He left when I was a year and a half, not two,
because when I was two,
she moved to Detroit because she'd heard,
he moved there.
But he didn't move.
He came over with a shotgun,
an' took my sister and I outa her mamma and papa's house.

Maybe that's why I was so scared of him when I was eight,
'n maybe I remembered,
            maybe I remembered him somewhere in my gut
pointing that shot-gun,
and say'n he was go'n to take his kids home,
come what may.

So now, if you'd ask me about my father I'd say:
"Maybe he knew my mother's papa was a child molester,
maybe that's why he came with that shot-gun.

I sorta wished I'da saved that letter—
maybe if I could read it now,
I could learn more about him.
You know, I'd sorta like to know more."

Found And Lost

Her mind is on my mind.

Her reality moving along like a wind-up toy
       in need of another good turn—
has changed its focus,
hopped on a train
a fast train
to an empty time,
a hollow place—

landscape reduced to wind.

Her mind is left behind.

It's left on the seat,
an old paperback book
she knew so well for so long
that she now picks up and rips out
page after page after page—
the same page,
and the one before—
just disappears them into dust.

Or Two

I don't have Alzheimer's like my Mother
but I might as well
the way I deny reality.

Some would say that's a choice,
some blatant ignoring
some—fear.

Again I think of death too often
to make peace in my body.

There were times in my life I longed for it
so much so
I tried to help it along,
give it a hand
or two.

I was young,
blind-sided
short-sighted
very unhappy
lost and alone in spite of a body
lying next to me all night long—
or—
because of it.

Alone

I want
to make the demons keep their distance
at least for the rest of this night
and maybe until the next night (alone)
without you.

But I still at fifty-four
haven't captured
standing at the window
the way it feels to think
if only I were powerful enough
if only I were deserving enough
if only I were good enough
if only I were loved enough
you would appear like magic
when I felt I couldn't hold my own with the night much longer.

But she, my mother didn't when I was young,
and you my friend don't when I am this old
and so I see my blinding confusion
with magic and power.

4 A.M.

I collect my warm memories
hoard them in a safe place
to push the cold out on frigid nights
when I am old.

I hide them in a secret space
I hoard them in a sacred place
I lift them out as gently as picking up a newborn
one by one
with long intervals in between
to gather every morsel of warmth
they can provide.

I give myself these gifts
on cold, cold nights
when it is late and lonely
like pictures from the heart.

Soul Catcher

I lie here having my shoulder massaged
when what I really want is to scream no!
no! no! no! no! no!
What I need is a soul massage
can you find it?
because if I have to point out where the pain is
I sure as hell can't.

I sit here in the arbor
waiting for the pain to dissolve
my soul to return
but it doesn't.
I should have known the magic wouldn't be here
without the wisteria in bloom.
The mockingbird stirs my spirit
maybe it can sing my soul back to health
slip it into my body again.
Where does one look when you've lost it?
Why can't it be as easy as finding the misplaced
hammer or hand shovel?

I wake up for the third time tonight
my anxiety still keeping me company.
Should I get up and look for my soul
among the dust balls gathered in the corners of the room?
Maybe I could make a soul-catcher to hang over the bed here?
If there are dream-catchers
why not soul-catchers too?

They may be the same thing after all.

On Paper

Yeah, think I'll do it—
hang out that sign
gone fishing.

I'll just sit by the river
filled to the brim
with peace and jumping fish
and write you long
loving letters sent airmail
via heron.

The only fishing I want to do
will be with my heart and eyes.

I want to go West to the mountains
lie on my back at the foot of El Capitan.

When I am drenched with its beauty
I'll roll over on to my belly
and try to capture it with words
just for you.

Her Touch

I'm taken away from myself and into myself
by an amazing woman
a healer
a human spirit you seldom meet who turns your life around
shakes it up when you least expect it—

your defenses down

your spirit down

feeling like you have nowhere to go but

down and

down and

down and then:

along comes this amazing spirit with eyes
like you've never seen before
a blue lost on any lens,
a brilliant mouth
and hands almost too small to pull out a magic much larger,
she says,
than what they put in—
        giving you life back
        shifting all pain to a new unwallowing light

and reminding you
to remember this.

What All's in Mine

Ahhh….

I'd love to see what's in your pockets.
Then I'd really know you.

a small cracked package of oyster crackers and lint
a magic marker (purple)
an elephant bottle cap
one hair pin
two baggie ties (same pocket)
two Art Deco buttons (different pockets)
a Zippo lighter
a rectangle of cotton fabric with embroidered love birds cut from
a tattered pillowcase
the stone I found under the pecan tree in front of the house
I was born in—
a folded fortune from Szechuan West:

> "Life is a tragedy for those who feel
>   and a comedy for those who drink"

There.
And that's just my bathrobe.

Where Else?

I have lived a life, good and bad
sad and happy
not done with it quite yet
but it may have another opinion,
c'est la vie.

I've been left in the lurch more often
than I have liked.

I would love to be a bird, not an angel
and fly over our land,
beautiful land we had so much fun on,
love
work
and play and play and play
in ecstasy in this lifetime,
here and now,
where else?

Scarlet Colsen was born in Kellis Store, Mississippi, in 1939, but moved to Grosse Ile, Michigan when she was five. Shortly after high school, she was discovered by Oleg Casini and was invited to New York where she worked as a high-fashion model for ten years and earned the dubious distinction of being the first and only "Marlboro Woman". She also appeared in the "Mirror of Venus", a Sexist piece of pseudo-poetry conceived by Federico Fellini, Francoise Sagan and Wingate Paine. Since modeling is the epitome of oppressive objectification, Scarlet naturally embraced the ethics and politics of Radical Feminism. It was around this time that she began her first formal studies in sculpture. Shortly after, to explore the performance aspect of art, she studied acting with Gordon Phillips and Filmmaking at Columbia University. Scarlet co-wrote, co-directed, and acted in two short films. While all creative activities feed on each other and nourish us, by the mid-1980's, she began writing and sculpting in earnest, and in 1995, moved from Riverdale in the Bronx to New Paltz, NY. Her poetry has appeared in *Chronogram, Plough Quarterly Magazine,* and awostingalchemy.com. Her art has been shown in the Mid-Hudson Valley, Brooklyn, NY, and Cape Cod, MA. More recently, she appeared in an acclaimed regional production of "The Vagina Monologues". For several years now, Scarlet's been writing her life story.

She has the great good fortune to live on a river in paradise with the love of her life, and is just as lucky to have an incredible daughter and two amazing grandchildren.